To/ my dear friend, Birthday Girl Sue,

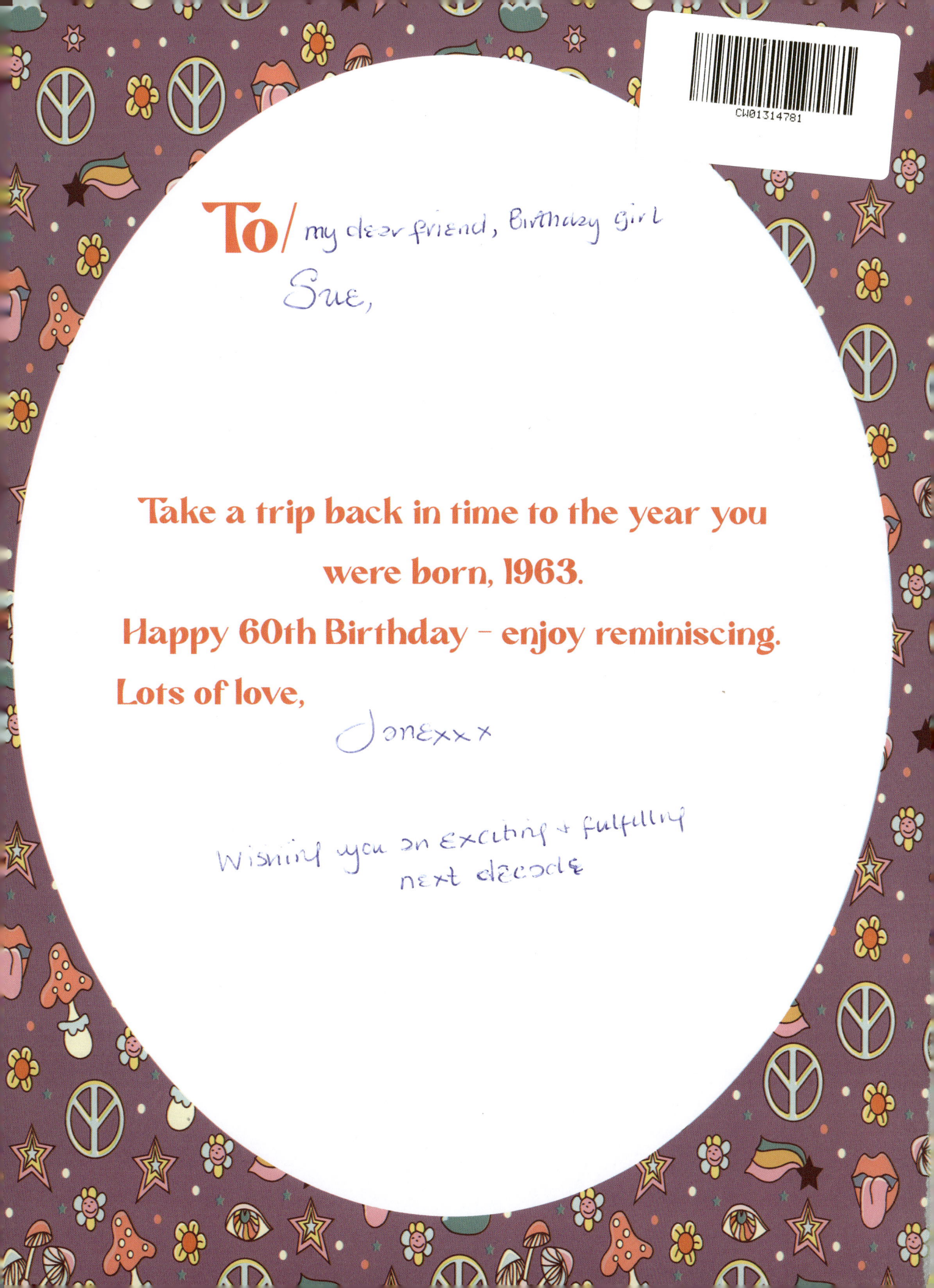

Take a trip back in time to the year you were born, 1963.

Happy 60th Birthday – enjoy reminiscing.

Lots of love,

JonExxx

Wishing you an exciting + fulfilling next decade

1963

We return to all the excitement of the swinging Sixties. A golden age for fashion, art, and music. A time of optimism and change around the world - mid-way through the decade, we can already see some of the exciting changes taking place. 1963 saw the country gripped by Beatlemania and your first winter was the coldest on record for over 20 years.

A peek into the everyday lives of people can be found in Popular Culture. This is a snapshot of life in 1963 and the culture of the time.

Best Picture was given to Lawrence of Arabia at the 35th Academy Awards. Beatlemania began in Britain on 22nd March, when the Beatles released their first album, Please Please Me. The group's second album, With the Beatles, replaces the group's first album, which topped the charts for 30 weeks.

An extremely publicised and salacious divorce occurred between the Duke and Duchess of Argyll in March 1963. The Duke hires an investigator to break into a locked cabinet while the Duchess is away from home. In the cabinet, nude photographs of his wife and another man, assumed to be Duncan Sandys, are found. The Sindy fashion doll makes its debut in stores. The Great Train Robbery took place in Buckinghamshire on 8 August. 15 robbers hijack a Royal Mail train between Glasgow and London, stealing over £2.6 million and fleeing to Leatherslade Farm. Most of the gang members would be arrested and convicted based on evidence recovered there.

Doctor Who debuts on BBC Television for the first time on 23 November. Edward Craven-Walker launches the Astro lava lamp, which goes on to enjoy widespread success in homes across the country.

The American Express credit card is introduced to the UK market. 69-year-old Prime Minister Harold Macmillan announces his resignation after seven years of service due to ill health. The worst winter in nearly 20 years hit Britain in 1963. Some areas have snow on the ground until April because of low temperatures.

You Have Been Loved for

60 years

Thats 720 months

3129 weeks | 21900 days

525600 hrs

31536000 minutes

1892160000 seconds

and counting...

60 YEARS AGO 1963

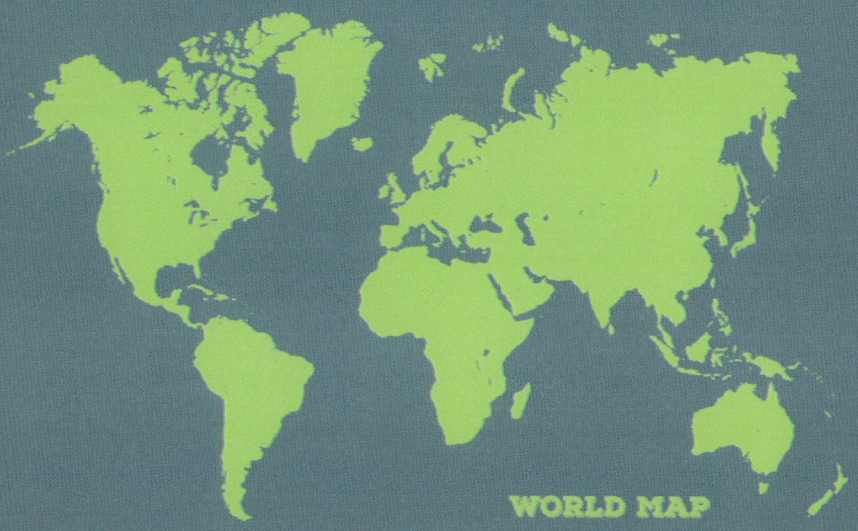
WORLD MAP

World Population

3.07 BILLION

Britain population

52.6 MILLION

2023 World Population

8 BILLION

Britain population

68.77 MILLION

MAJOR WORLD LEADERS

UK PRIME MINISTER- Harold Macmillan, Prime Minister of the United Kingdom (1957–1963) Sir Alec Douglas-Home - from 19 October onwards.

US PRESIDENT - John F. Kennedy, President of the United States (1961–1963) Lyndon B. Johnson - from November 22 onwards

RUSSIA/SOVIET UNION - Communist Party Leader - Nikita Khrushchev, First Secretary of the Communist Party of the Soviet Union (1953–1964)

SOUTH AFRICA - Prime Minister -- Hendrik Frensch Verwoerd

ITALY - Prime Minister - Amintore Fanfani, President of the Council of Ministers of Italy (1960–1963) Giovanni Leone --From 21 June to 4 December. Aldo Moro -- From 4 December onwards.

GERMANY - Chancellor -- Konrad Adenauer. Ludwig Erhard -- From 16 October

FRANCE -- President -- Charles de Gaulle

CANADA - Prime Minister - John Diefenbaker, (1957–1963). Lester B. Pearson -- from April 22

FRANCE - President - Charles de Gaulle, President of France (1959–1969)

Average cost of living 1963

- Average house price £3,160
- Ford Cortina car £675
- 19" Philips dual standard black & white TV (Currys) 69 guineas
- Hoover Constellation 862 vacuum cleaner £19 12s 6d
- Rolls-Colston Mk IV dishwasher £78 15s
- Russell Hobbs K2 electric kettle £5 5s
- Lec F160 chest freezer £103 9s 7d
- Servis Supertwin - washing machine (Currys) 77 guineas
- Axminster carpet per square yard 82s
- Morphy-Richards TOS toaster £5 18s 6d
- Gallon of petrol 4s 9d

Pint of beer 2s 1d
20 cigarettes 4s 6d
Pint of milk 8½d
Pepsi Cola (Spar) 2s 6d

Cinema ticket - 3s 1d

Records
45 rpm single cost about 6s 8d, and an LP £1 12s 6d

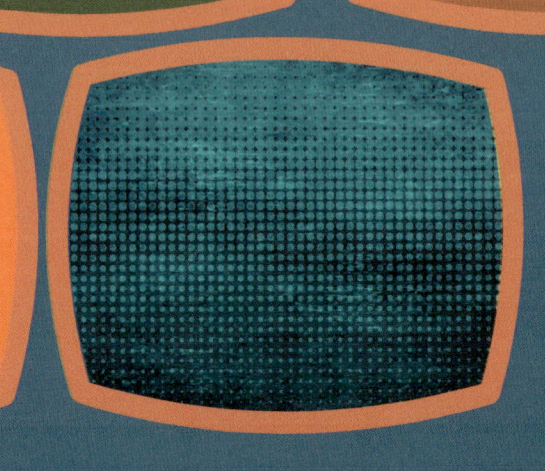

Did You Know?

On March 21st 1963 Alcatraz Prison closed its doors after 29 years in operation in San Francisco Bay. A decision to close the prison wasn't made because Morris and the Anglins disappeared (the decision to shut down was made long before they were missing), but due to its high operating costs.

Even though it hasn't been open for years, Alcatraz is a famous prison in the United States. As a result of its location on an island separated from the mainland, it developed quite a reputation for itself over time. Over the past few decades, it has been the subject of stories that have turned into nightmares throughout the entire country and around the world.

Martin Luther King Jr. delivered the speech "I Have a Dream" during the March on Washington for Jobs and Freedom on August 28, 1963. During his speech, King advocated for civil and economic rights in the United States and the end of racism. A defining moment in the civil rights movement and one of the most iconic speeches in American history, the Lincoln Memorial speech was delivered to over 250,000 supporters.

A crazy conspiracy emerged in which Bob Dylan stole Blowin' in the Wind from a New Jersey high-school student named Lorre Wyatt.

Thich Quang Duc's self-immolation caused many Americans to question their involvement in Vietnam.

The Supreme Court ruled on June 17 that laws requiring students to recite the Lord's Prayer or Bible verses in school were unconstitutional.

Gaylord Perry remarked in 1963 that they would put a man on the moon before he hits a home run. On July 20, 1969, a few hours after Neil Armstrong stepped onto the moon, Perry hit his only home run.

Boxer Sonny Liston, who defeated Floyd Patterson in Chicago on September 25th, became the first person to win a million dollars from a single fight.

50 & Famous

- **Michael Jordan** - "Air Jordan" was a high-flying Chicago Bulls shooting guard who was considered one of the greatest basketball players in history. His six NBA titles, six NBA Finals MVPs, and five NBA MVPs make him the most decorated player in NBA history.

- **Johnny Depp** - Known for his role as Captain Jack Sparrow in the Pirates of the Caribbean film franchise. He is also known for his roles in Edward Scissorhands, Ed Wood, Donnie Brasco, Blow, and What's Eating Gilbert Grape. For his role in Sweeney Todd: The Demon Barber of Fleet Street, he was awarded a Golden Globe for Best Actor.

- **Whitney Houston** - With hits such as "Hold Me" from her record-breaking self-titled album, she became the most awarded female singer in history. A musical family surrounded her, including her cousin Dionne Warwick and godmother Aretha Franklin.

- **Brad Pitt** - He has starred in acclaimed films such as Moneyball, Fight Club, The Curious Case of Benjamin Button, World War Z, and Inglourious Basterds. In the Ocean's Eleven trilogy, he played Rusty Ryan. In the 2019 film Once Upon a Time in Hollywood, he was nominated for an Academy Award for Best Supporting Actor.

- **Lisa Kudrow** - She gained fame as Phoebe Buffay on NBC's Friends from 1994 to 2004. In recognition of her work, she was awarded a Satellite Award for Best Actress and a Screen Actors Guild Award for Best Actress. In addition to writing and producing, she starred in the HBO series The Comeback.

MOVIES

The Great Escape

Police in the German town where this movie was filmed set up a speed trap near the set one day. The cast and crew, including Steve McQueen, were caught. McQueen was arrested and briefly jailed after the Chief of Police told him: "Herr McQueen, we have caught several of your comrades today, but you have won the prize (for the highest speeding)."

John Cairney and Nigel Green did not like working together. In their last scene together, Hercules and Hylas explore the treasure chamber hidden on the pedestal of the mighty Talos. As a result of the extremely bright lighting used to make the treasure sparkle, the actors began losing their vision the following day. After becoming temporarily blind, they were both bandaged for two weeks in the same hospital room. Their common interests led them to quickly become friends.

From Russia with Love

Former President John F. Kennedy ranked Ian Fleming's novel among his top ten favorite novels. Life Magazine published that list on March 17, 1961. This may have influenced the producers' decision to make this the second James Bond movie. In November 1963, during a private screening at the White House, this was the last movie J.F.K. ever saw, according to "Death of a President" by William Raymond Manchester.

Films 1963

- **The Great Escape** - Director: John Sturges | Stars: Steve McQueen, James Garner, Richard Attenborough, Charles Bronson
- **Charade** - Director: Stanley Donen | Stars: Cary Grant, Audrey Hepburn, Walter Matthau, James Coburn
- **Cleopatra** - Director: Joseph L. Mankiewicz | Stars: Elizabeth Taylor, Richard Burton, Rex Harrison, Pamela Brown
- **The Pink Panther** - Director: Blake Edwards | Stars: David Niven, Peter Sellers, Robert Wagner, Capucine
- **The Birds** - Director: Alfred Hitchcock | Stars: Rod Taylor, Tippi Hedren, Jessica Tandy, Suzanne Pleshette
- **From Russia with Love** - Director: Terence Young | Stars: Sean Connery, Robert Shaw, Lotte Lenya, Daniela Bianchi
- **McLintock!** - Director: Andrew V. McLaglen | Stars: John Wayne, Maureen O'Hara, Patrick Wayne, Stefanie Powers
- **It's a Mad Mad Mad Mad World** - Director: Stanley Kramer | Stars: Spencer Tracy, Milton Berle, Ethel Merman, Mickey Rooney
- **Federico Fellini's 8½** - Director: Federico Fellini | Stars: Marcello Mastroianni, Anouk Aimée, Claudia Cardinale, Sandra Milo
- **Bye Bye Birdie** - Director: George Sidney | Stars: Dick Van Dyke, Ann-Margret, Janet Leigh, Maureen Stapleton
- **Donovan's Reef** - Director: John Ford | Stars: John Wayne, Lee Marvin, Betty Ellen, Jack Warden
- **Murder at the Gallop** - Director: George Pollock | Stars: Margaret Rutherford, Stringer Davis, Robert Morley, Flora Robson
- **Jason and the Argonauts** - Director: Don Chaffey | Stars: Todd Armstrong, Nancy Kovack, Gary Raymond, Laurence Naismith

MUSIC

Each decade has a distinct sound and memorable music that defines the age and becomes part of people's lives through shared memories. The 1960s stood out more than any other. There is no way to succinctly describe the music scene of the 60s in a way that adequately reflects its impact on those who came of age during this time. Despite its beginnings in the 1950s, rock music really came of age in the 1960s. Almost everyone today knows the biggest bands of the 1960s, including The Beatles, The Rolling Stones, The Velvet Underground, The Who, The Doors, Frank Zappa, Jimi Hendrix, Led Zeppelin, The Kinks, Pink Floyd, The Beach Boys, The Kinks, and many more. Artists throughout every decade since have been influenced by these huge bands.

Born in 1963, you'll remember the excitement of visiting a record shop and finding that song you've been dying to listen to. As you crowded your room with your friends, the first few notes from your vinyl player filled the room with emotion like you hadn't experienced before. Although the benefits of technology are plentiful, for example, thousands of tracks are available for download instantly. It is difficult to imagine a streaming service having the same effect.

No.1

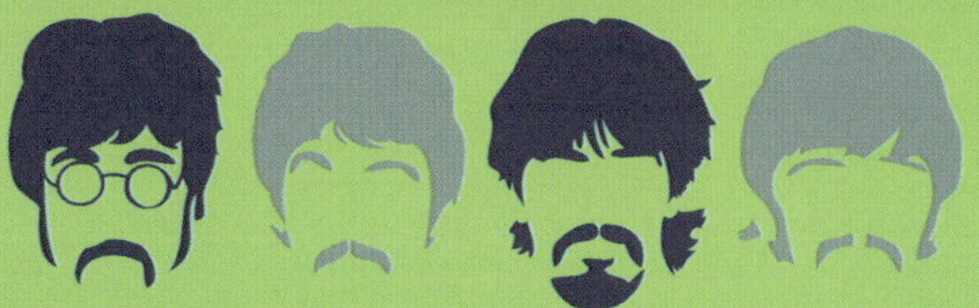

What was the number 1 on the day you were born? Look at the table below to find out.

21.01.63	Cliff Richard and The Shadows	The Next Time
28.02.63	The Shadows	Dance On!
18.02.63	Jet Harris and Tony Meehan	Diamonds
11.03.63	Frank Ifield	Wayward Wind
25.03.63	Cliff Richard and The Shadows	Summer Holiday
01.04.63	The Shadows	Foot Tapper
08.04.63	Cliff Richard and The Shadows	Summer Holiday (2nd time)
29.04.63	Gerry and The Pacemakers	How Do You Do It
27.06.63	The Beatles	From Me To You
15.07.63	Gerry and The Pacemakers	I Like It
29.07.63	Frank Ifield	Confessin
05.08.63	Elvis Presley	Devil In Disguise
19.08.63	The Searchers	Sweets For My Sweet
09.09.63	Billy J. Kramer and The Dakotas	Bad To Me
07.10.63	The Beatles	She Loves You
28.10.63	Brian Poole and The Tremeloes	Do You Love Me
25.11.63	Gerry and The Pacemakers	You'll Never Walk Alone
09.12.63	The Beatles	She Loves You (2nd time)
31.12.63	The Beatles	I Want To Hold Your Hand

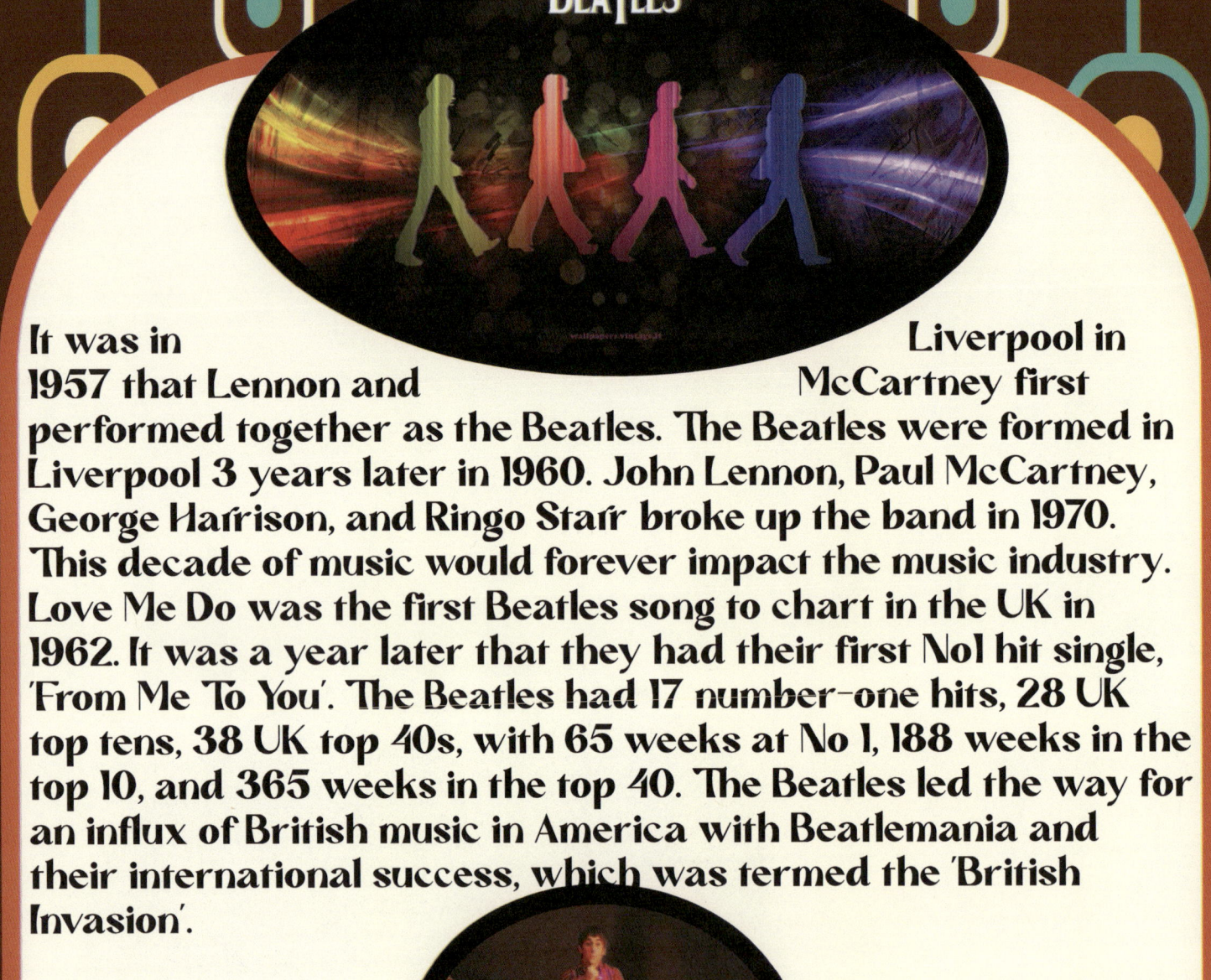

It was in 1957 that Lennon and McCartney first performed together as the Beatles. Liverpool in The Beatles were formed in Liverpool 3 years later in 1960. John Lennon, Paul McCartney, George Harrison, and Ringo Starr broke up the band in 1970. This decade of music would forever impact the music industry. Love Me Do was the first Beatles song to chart in the UK in 1962. It was a year later that they had their first No1 hit single, 'From Me To You'. The Beatles had 17 number-one hits, 28 UK top tens, 38 UK top 40s, with 65 weeks at No 1, 188 weeks in the top 10, and 365 weeks in the top 40. The Beatles led the way for an influx of British music in America with Beatlemania and their international success, which was termed the 'British Invasion'.

In 1964, The Who was formed in London. It was formed by Pete Townshend, bass guitarist and singer John Entwistle, and drummer Keith Moon. Globally, they have sold more than 100 million records. Despite this success, they haven't had a UK No 1 single (though an album has reached the top spot). With 43 weeks in the top 10s and 194 weeks in the top 40s, they have had 14 top 10s and 25 top 40s in the UK.

Pink Floyd

Pink Floyd formed in London in 1965. Gaining an early following as one of the first British psychedelic groups, Pink Floyd were founded by students Syd Barrett (guitar, lead vocals), Nick Mason (drums), Roger Waters (bass guitar, vocals), and Richard Wright (keyboards, vocals).

Pink Floyd are one of the greatest progressive rock bands of all time. The Dark Side of the Moon and The Wall are among the best-selling albums of all time, and both have been inducted into the Grammy Hall of Fame. However, despite all their success to date In the UK they have had just 1 single to hit the UK No 1 spot, however they did have 6 No 1 albums. The group have sold over 250 million albums worldwide.

The Rolling Stones

In 1962, the Stones injected grit into 60s pop rock. As one of the most successful artists of all time, they have sold an estimated 240 million records. Their inclusion in the Rock and Roll Hall of Fame in 1989 and later in the UK Hall of Fame in 2004 was a direct result of this recognition. The band has released a staggering 30 albums to date! As well as three Grammys, they have received a Grammy lifetime achievement award.

Revolution

It was the counterculture of the 60s that sparked the anti-establishment movement that spread throughout Western society. Tensions grew around sexuality, women's rights, civil rights, and authority figures and establishments in the UK and Western countries around the mid-60s, resulting in various sub-cultures.

The subcultures offered the world completely different perspectives on all aspects of life by expressing creativity and pushing the boundaries of 'accepted norms.' All aspects of life were affected by this bubbling creative movement, which helped shape ideas, concepts, and movements that changed everyday life for the better. Throughout mainstream society, this challenge to the accepted 'norms' led to a 'revolution' that affected fashion, music, sexuality, and in general the everyday lives of normal families.

Opposition to these changes in society was based on concerns that they reflected the decay and destruction of society. Unstoppable expansion and dreams of a better future quelled this disquieting voice.

Vietnam War & Civil Rights in America

In his election campaign, John F. Kennedy focused on the "New Frontier", a series of reforms designed to deal with injustices and inequalities in society. In his campaign, he successfully captured the people's thirst for change. A number of challenges and government failures (the Cuban Missile Crisis and Bay of Pigs fiasco) plagued him early on, and he failed to galvanise his party to make the change that he had promised. In 1964, President Kennedy was assassinated. These reforms were also promised by his successor, but the government was left with scarce resources due to the financial costs of the Vietnam War. There were a lot of protests by young people against the war. Some even fled their homes in order to avoid conscription.

President Johnson authored the Civil Rights Act of 1964, which prohibited discrimination in public places. The following year, the Voting Rights Act was amended to remove any barriers to voting. Black power became the new focus of civil rights groups during the mid-60s as a result of a lack of government reform. In order to incite change, activists grew more radical. People wanted authentic change, but the revolution faced many challenges. The assassinations of Martin Luther King Jr. and Bobby Kennedy took place in 1968. The realisation that America would not win the Vietnam War contributed to the end of the optimism present at the beginning of the decade.

The pop art movement originated in the 1950s and became synonymous with the 1960s. Originally conceived in Britain and America, it inspired artists from all over the world to participate. This was a reflection of society's changes, particularly among young people who were challenging many traditions and expectations. Pop art, Hamilton wrote in 1957, consists of Popularity (designed to appeal to a broad audience), Transient (short-term solutions), Expendability (easy to forget), and low cost (mass-produced, young, witty, sexy, gimmicky, glamorous, and big business). In pop art history, Andy Warhol's canned soup image is widely known. His art pieces were inspired by everyday media and consumer products. It was in 1962 that he first exhibited Campbell's soup.

Pop Art

POPULAR 60S TV SHOWS

The BBC has broadcast Doctor Who since 1963. Since 1963, Doctor Who has been a popular science fiction show, lasting until 1989, then from 2005 to the present.

A BBC sitcom about the Home Guard, a British militia. It ran for nine series and 80 episodes from 1968 to 1977.

In 1960, Coronation Street premiered and is still one of Britain's most popular soap operas.

Thunderbirds Thunderbirds are go! A marionette animated series by Gerry and Sylvia Anderson ran from 1965 to 1966

It wasn't just music that was influenced by the British invasion. The spy craze led to British television productions appearing on American networks. These shows were produced in the United Kingdom for primetime broadcast in America.

- With 161 episodes, The Avengers was an espionage television show created in 1961 until 1969.
- Based on John Creasey's books, the Baron series was made in 1965 and 1966
- An espionage thriller/science fiction/occult detective fiction adventure, The Champions, It consists of 30 episodes broadcast on the UK network ITV between 1968 and 1969.
- Journey to the Unknown aired on ABC from 1968 to 1969 and then aired in the UK on ITV during 1969.
- Lew Grade's ITC Entertainment produced the private eye thriller series Man in a Suitcase. From 27 September 1967 until 17 April 1968, it aired on ITV in the United Kingdom.
- An unnamed British intelligence agent is abducted and imprisoned in a mysterious coastal village in 1967's The Prisoner, a British avant-garde television series about social science fiction.
- During the 1960s and 1970s, the British ITC aired the mystery spy thriller The Saint.
- The British television series Secret Agent aired between 1960 and 1962.

Adverts in the '60s

The 1960s saw the transition from black & white line drawings to full colour photography in advertisements. Advertisements in the U.S. were ahead of those in the UK. American ads from the '50s were used as artistic inspiration in U.K ads from the '60s.

Advertisers often refer to the 1960s as the 'Golden Age' of advertising since it was bright, modern, and cool compared to previous generations. With the advent of colour TV, advertisers were able to create campaigns that would not only advertise their product but also contribute to the cultural landscape. It is not uncommon for television commercials to transport people back in time with the same significance and effect as personal family memories. People enjoyed advertisements in the 1960s because they were novel, fun, and offered good information about products. Of course, life has changed in the modern era, partly due to the sheer amount of advertising and data tracking we are exposed to, as well as privacy concerns.

A cultural & social analysis of vintage advertisements:

Buy British is a campaign that dates back to the 1960s. Heatonex's advert on the following page illustrates how adverts use the association with British quality and craftsmanship.

During the 1960s and 1980s, Jean Tyrell ran Sirdar and turned it into an international brand. She doubled profits in her first year by adding patterns to the company's line. An example of how images and patterns effectively sell a product can be found on the following page.

Advertisements promoting Leisure products demonstrate how stereotypes were adopted by advertising agencies. Housewife delighted at husband's thoughtful purchase! Alongside this is the "Dinner at 8 is a new world" advert. Advertising was used by kitchen and homeware appliance suppliers to ensure that their products were seen at the forefront of the post-war economic boom and demand for convenience technology.

Analysing advertisements can also reveal changes in our eating habits. In the 1960s, more convenient cereals replaced traditional English breakfasts. Kellogg's slogan promises "the best to you everyday". Convenience foods were a must-have during the '60s. An advert for Walls emphasised the freshness of the products available in their local store. At the time, supermarkets were still relatively new, and suppliers used advertising to make sure consumers were happy with the quality and freshness. Using products that make life easier - the JIF advert and the Walls desserts - to illustrate the changing habits of shoppers.

Up until the late 1950s, wall-to-wall carpeting was a privilege reserved for the wealthy. As manufacturing advances reduced costs, carpets became more popular in all types of households. It was not uncommon for 1960s and 1970s homes to have wall-to-wall carpet in the bathrooms! The Naylor advertisement (Woman & Home original advertisement from the early '60s) suggests that a bold pattern carpet would be just the thing for a trendy young couple to furnish their new home. A colour bathroom suite was also a popular trend, as indicated by the original advertisement below from Shires that claimed "the elegance...the luxury...".

At the beginning of the decade, childrenswear followed the traditional miniature version of adult clothing as was prevalent in previous decades. As adult fashion evolved with new technologies, everything changed. Children's clothing advertisements from Ladybird, Dolly Mixture and Birthday show early adoption of bold, bright colours and styles.

Even Skuff Kote's advertisement tells a story. Shoeshine boys declined in the 1960s, and they are now a thing of the past in most Western countries. The introduction of convenience products changed people's way of life as the economy grew along with technological advancements. In the advertisement, children's shoes are shown to look new despite wear and tear from playful children. Throughout this decade, convenience has been the key message behind many products.

Birthday
SHOES and SANDALS
the next best thing to bare foot freedom
modern styling, superb quality, reliable wear ...you get so much more with
Birthday
SHOES & SANDALS
FOR CHILDREN OF ALL AGES
"The best to you each morning"
Kellogg's
Best taste
Best nourishment
Best value
CORN FLAKES
CRISP and FULL OF SUN
"Buy Heatonex" says Cathy, "they're British through and through".
Yes she's right, Heatonex school coats have an extra feel of style and quality, a British product through and through with that traditional quality of finish and material.
Mums know it too. They wear so well that the generous let-down comes in handy.
Style choice is the sophisticated raglan stroller, or regular style (with zip safety purse). Colours – Navy, Royal, Green, Brown, Maroon, Grey, to fit all ages.
Don't forget Cathy, Heatonex make a smashing duffel coat too.
GABERDINE SCHOOLCOATS
Heatonex
HEATONS (LEEDS) LIMITED
NEW MILL LANE, CLIFFORD, BOSTON SPA, YORKSHIRE
Jif
3 thrilling flavours in the Wall's 1/6 size
Wall's
Wall's foods reach your shop as fresh as your daily pinta!
Fresh delivery–just one of the five good reasons why
SIRDAR
shires

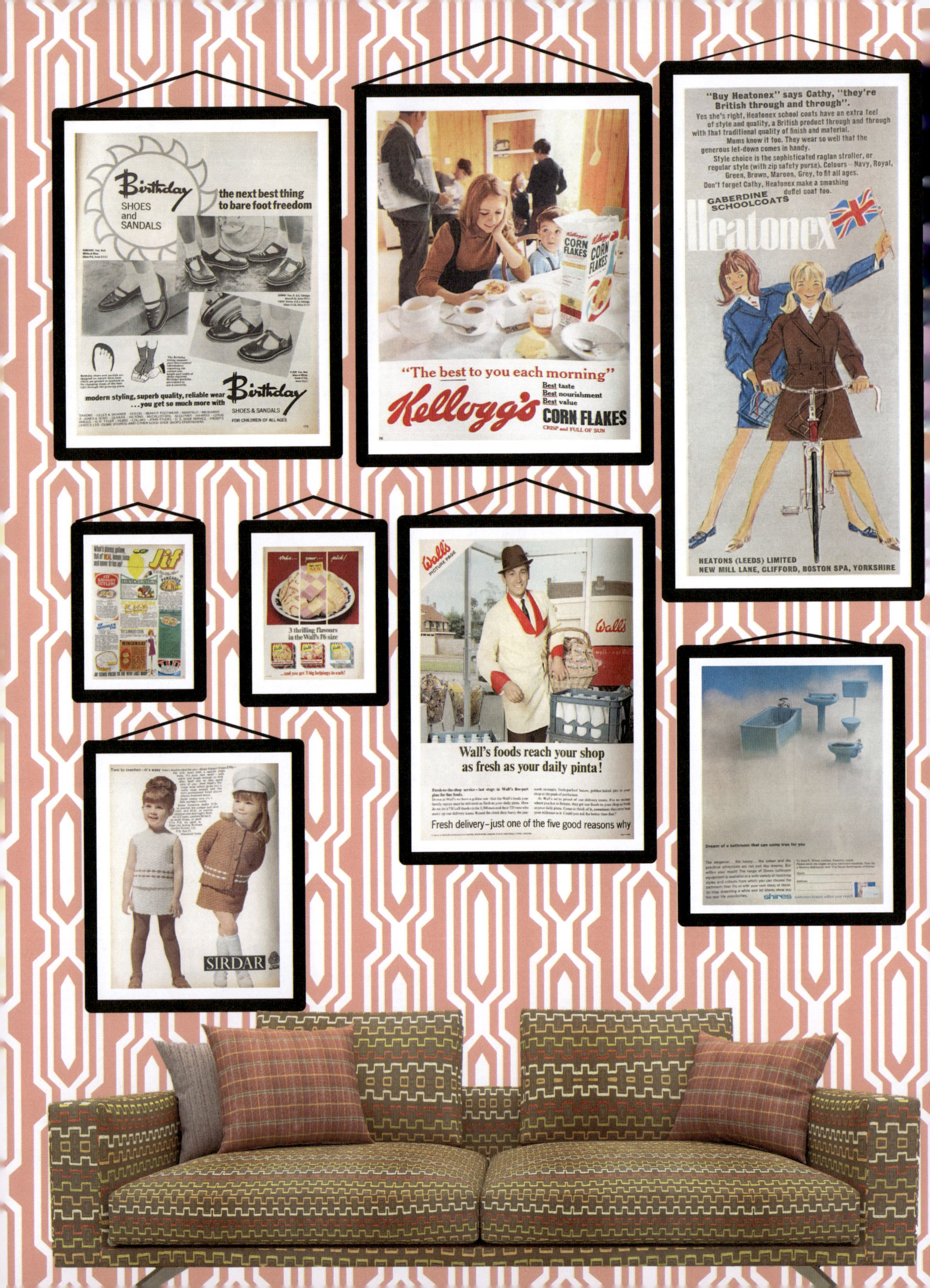

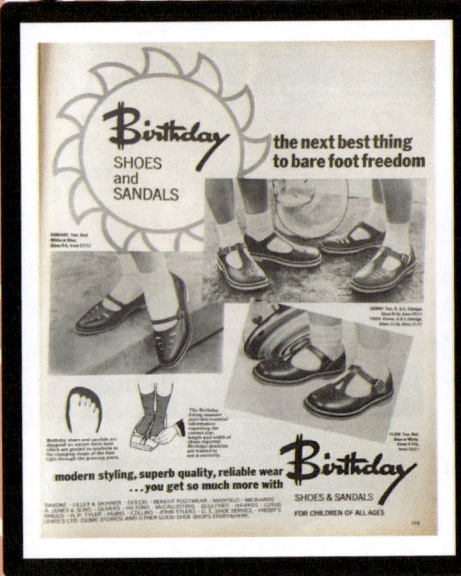

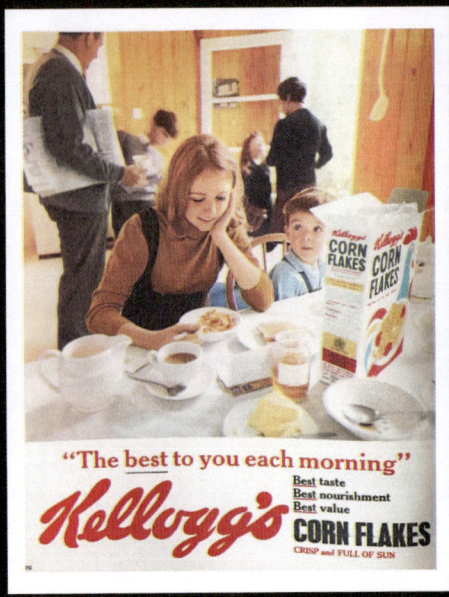

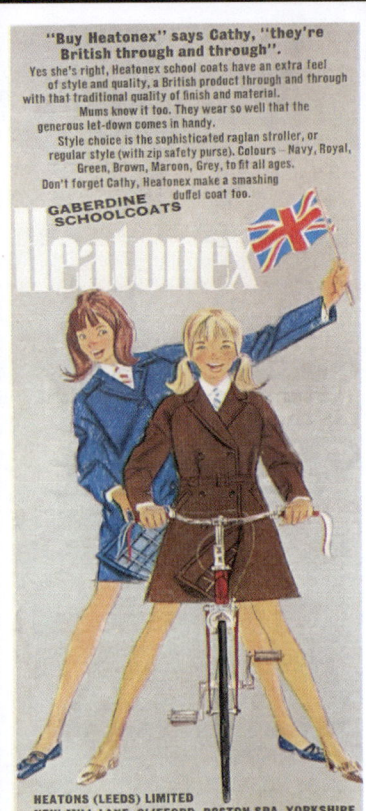

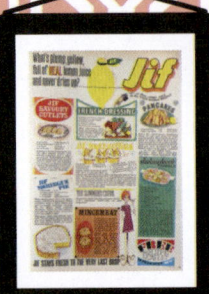

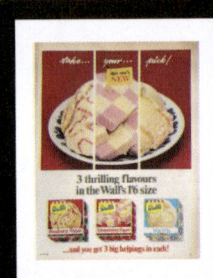

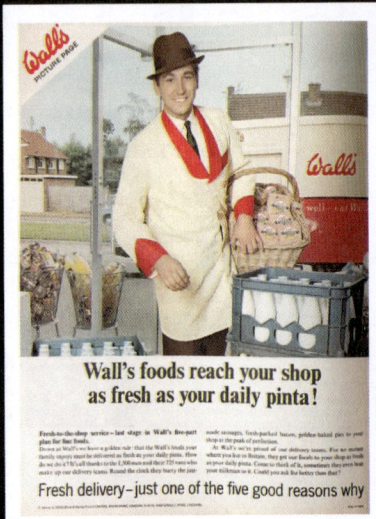

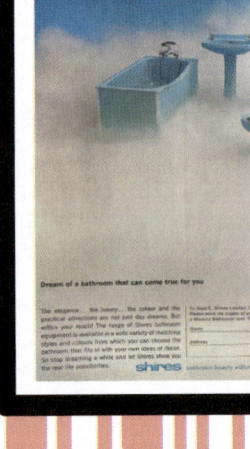

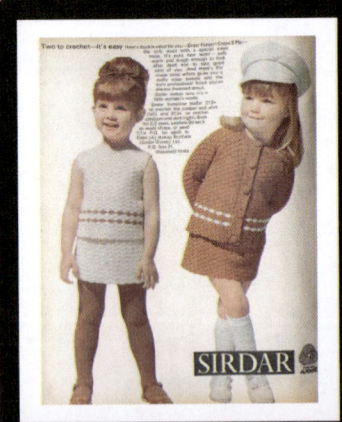

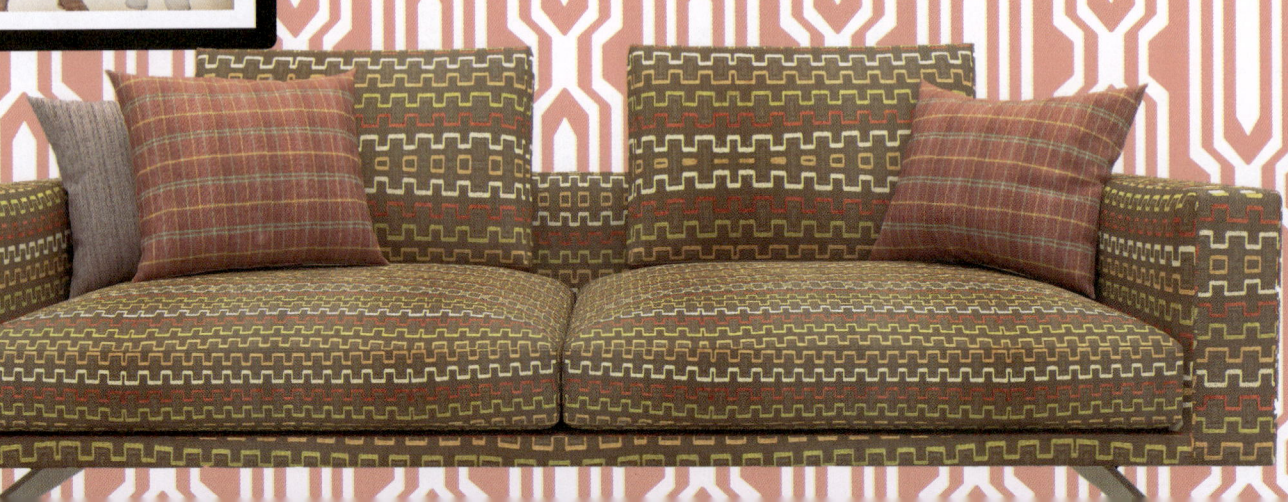

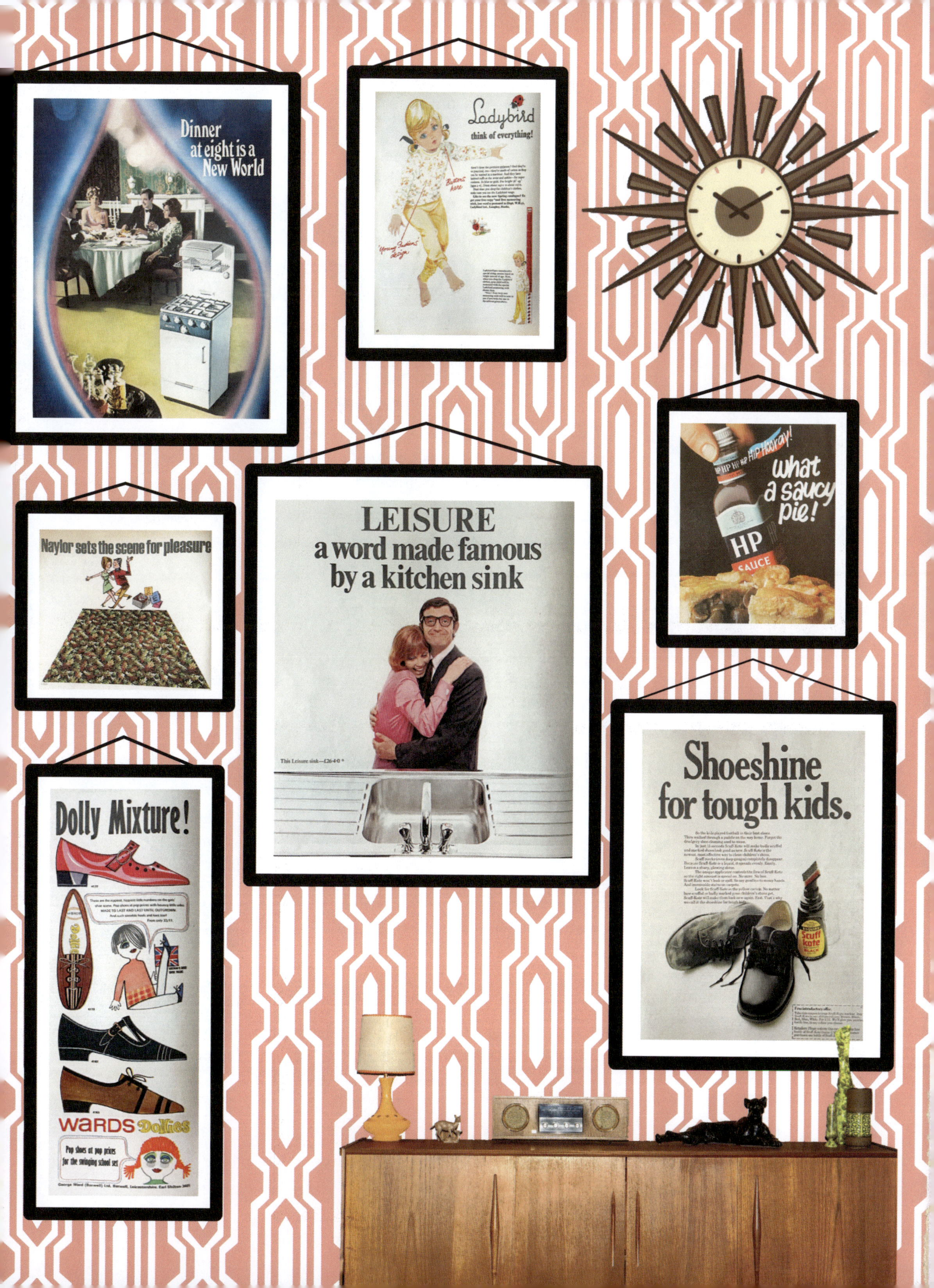

Fashion

In the 1960s, fashion became much more relaxed and casual. Across all age groups and genders, this trend was observed. A number of themes encapsulate the styles of the 60s; Jackie O's style and the ladylike elegance continued from the 50's, with boundary-pushing styles from designers such as Mary Quant along with space age influences, and of course the "hippie style". Menswear changed from the standard uniform and limited choices of the 50's. The men's fashion industry suddenly accepted patterns, textures, and colours normally reserved for women's clothing. Changes in society were reflected in the changing boundaries of fashion. In Britain, a number of trends were popularised by the media attention paid to small groups of young people within cities. Mini-skirts, culottes, go-go boots, PVC clothing, and other experimental styles were examples of these novel styles. Mary Quant's mini skirts, Jackie Kennedy's pillbox hat, and Twiggy's huge doe eyes with false lashes defined the 1960s 'look'. Similarly, hairstyles followed the experimental line, and the latest styles and lengths followed fashion trends. The hippie movement was characterised by psychedelic prints, neon colours, and mismatched patterns with floral motifs. During the early and mid-60's, 'Modernists' or 'Mods' were the biggest fashion influence on young men. As music and fashion intertwined, they reflected the desires of each subculture.

1960s Fashion

Fashion trends of the decade

- Oversized buttons on 2 piece skirt suits.

- Bright patterns and bold colours with raised hemlines.

- Women's knitted dresses & men's V-neck jumpers were hugely popular.

- Jumpers with ribbed cuffs and knit pleats in block colours. Accessorise with large chunky accessories.

- It was particularly fashionable to wear Peter Pan collars, psychedelic prints, and above-the-knee hemlines

- Brightly coloured wool coats with matching hats.

- Throughout the decade, dog tooth patterns were a hit.

- The short gamine crop or bee hive hair.

1960s TOYS

1961: Barbie finally has a boyfriend, Ken, who is exactly half an inch taller than her. It was a dilemma for Mattel. Should Ken be anatomically correct below the waist? It was solved by some non-removable 'perma-pants'.

Just behind Noddy, Scalextric enjoyed a boom year in 1961, when it was the third best-selling toy.

In 1962, Mousetrap was introduced with its catchphrase 'It's fun to build this comical wonder, but woe to the mouse who gets caught under it'. In 1962, Airfix was one of the most popular toys of the year due to its kit model construction

The Sindy doll was marketed as 'the doll you love to dress.' She flew off the shelves for Christmas in 1963. Matchbox's Diplomacy, a board game that requires cunning and skill, was a top seller

In 1964, MR Potato got a brand-new plastic body to replace his real potato body. During Beatlemania, toy dolls of the Beatles were also a huge hit.

1965: Aston Martin Aston Martin Car awarded for the first time. Children around the world aspired to become 007 as a result of the spy movie craze.

1966: Action Man becomes Britain's first doll for boys. The Spirograph was one of this year's most popular new toys. Doodling for hours of fun.

Toy classics from 1967. Kerplunk, Etch-a-Sketch, and wargames. Christmas lists were topped by battleships.

In 1968, Sindy dolls were more popular than Barbies and won the toy of the year award. Snoopy was a hugely popular Fisher Price toy that can be seen in many Christmas photos with toddlers who delighted pulling him along on his plastic lead. The Batman utility belt was the accessory of choice for slightly older boys.

Hot Wheels cars have consistently ranked among kids' favorite toys since the 1960s. Maybe the only difference is that it is now it is the top choice for both girls and boys, which wasn't the case in the 1960's.

Do you remember?

Popular 60s Children's TV shows

Biggles - a 1960s television series based on the Biggles series of books by W.E. Johns. Neville Whiting starred in the show.

Animal Magic - a BBC children's television series which ran from 1962 to 1983 from BBC. It began fortnightly moving to weekly in 1964.

Belle and Sebastian is a 1965 French TV children's serial based on the 1965 novel Belle et Sébastien by Cécile Aubry. It was 13 episodes long and starred Aubry's son Mehdi as Sebastien.

Bizzy Lizzy - a British children's TV series from the 1960s. Bizzy Lizzy was a little girl whose dress had a magic flower. When she touched it, her wishes came true — but if she made more than four wishes in a day, all her previous wishes were undone. Her first wish each day was to make her Eskimo doll, Little Mo, come to life.

Bleep and Booster - a children's cartoon series by William Timym (pronounced Tim) originally shown on the BBC's Blue Peter. A total of 313 five-minute episodes were released between 1964 and 1977.

Camberwick Green - a British children's television series that ran from January to March 1966 on BBC1, featuring stop motion puppets. Camberwick Green is the first in the Trumptonshire trilogy, which also includes Trumpton and Chigley.

Crackerjack - aired every year from 1955 to 1984 with the exception of 1971. You'll likely have strong memories of this popular kids variety show.

The Clangers is a stop-motion animation cartoon about a group of mouse like creatures who live on the moon. They converse in a whistle like voice and eat only green soup and blue string pudding (prepared by the Soup Dragon).

Do you remember?

- Trumpton 1967 BBC1
- Pingwings 1961-64
- Magpie 1968 ITV
- Watch with Mother 1952-1975
- Crackerjack 1955-1984
- The Herbs 1968
- Jackanory 1965-1996
- Blue Peter 1958 - present day. Longest running kids TV programme in the world

World Events 1963

The Kennedy assassination in the United States

Assassination of President John F Kennedy in the United States

In 1963, Lyndon Baines Johnson's commission, The Warren Commission, which investigated the death of the President for ten months, concluded that Lee Harvey Oswald killed the President alone. He also concluded that Jack Ruby killed him alone before he was charged.

Hurricane Flora in the Caribbean

On September 26th, a tropical depression formed near the Cape Verde Islands that developed into hurricane Flora. On September 30th, it was officially designated a hurricane and named Flora.

According to reports, between 6,000 and 8,000 people died, making it one of the deadliest hurricanes in the 20th century. It also did millions of dollars worth of damage and destroyed thousands of homes and buildings throughout the Caribbean.

The Early Years of Beatlemania

Between 1963 and 1969, each change in the Beatles' music style was accepted and embraced by their fans.

"Please Please Me" was the Beatles' first full-length album. It took the Beatles a single day to record their first full-length album at the end of February. The album included both original Paul McCartney and John Lennon songs and popular covers, and it was titled Please Please Me after their single. It was released in March of that year and topped the charts in the United Kingdom for thirty weeks until another Beatles album, "With The Beatles," took its place. The album included songs such as "I Saw Her Standing There," "Love Me Do," and "Twist and Shout."

The introduction of ZIP codes in the United States

In July 1963, the United States Postal Service launched the ZIP Code System.Developed in the United States to improve mail delivery efficiency, ZIP stands for "Zoning Improvement Plan".USPS expanded distribution centres and began assigning a five-digit code to every address before the ZIP code was introduced.There are different geographical markers associated with each digit in a ZIP code, with the top digit representing a general region in the U.S., the second and third representing sections of the country, and the last two representing a local post office or postal zone.

Mariner 2 Mission Ends

Mariner 2 lost contact with NASA on January 3rd, ending its successful mission. August 27, 1962, was the launch date for the Mariner 2 spacecraft. When it flew past Venus in December 1962, it became the first mission to observe another planet successfully. In the period before contact was lost, Venus' temperature, atmosphere, magnetic field, and radiation were transmitted back to Earth.

Civil Rights Act

The governor of Alabama faced General Henry Graham on June 12, 1963, at the University of Alabama in Tuscaloosa. African-American students James Hood and Vivian Malone were denied enrolment by Wallace. The Governor appointed himself the temporary registrar of the University, ignoring an order of the federal court, and blocked students from registering. President Kennedy responded by federalising the Alabama National Guard. George Wallace was ordered to "step aside" by his commander, General Henry Graham, as 100 guardsmen escorted the students to campus. In a speech on June 11, Kennedy clarified his position on civil rights. As a result of the bill he submitted to Congress, the Civil Rights Act of 1964 was passed.

Yugoslavia declares President Tito President for Life.

In April, the nation of Yugoslavia was transformed into the Socialist Federal Republic of Yugoslavia, with Josip Broz Tito serving as its "President for Life." As part of several socialist reforms adopted during that year, the name of the European nation and Tito's authority was changed. He encouraged foreign tourism and the expansion of private enterprise by easing many religious and political restrictions with his increased power. People admired Tito for standing against Soviet-era communism and developing a successful form of socialism. Tito died in 1980, and the Socialist Federal Republic of Yugoslavia ended in 1992.

The Profumo Scandal in the UK

As a result of the Profumo Crisis in the UK, war minister John Profumo resigned his cabinet post due to having an affair with Christina Wheeler, who also had a relationship with a Soviet naval officer

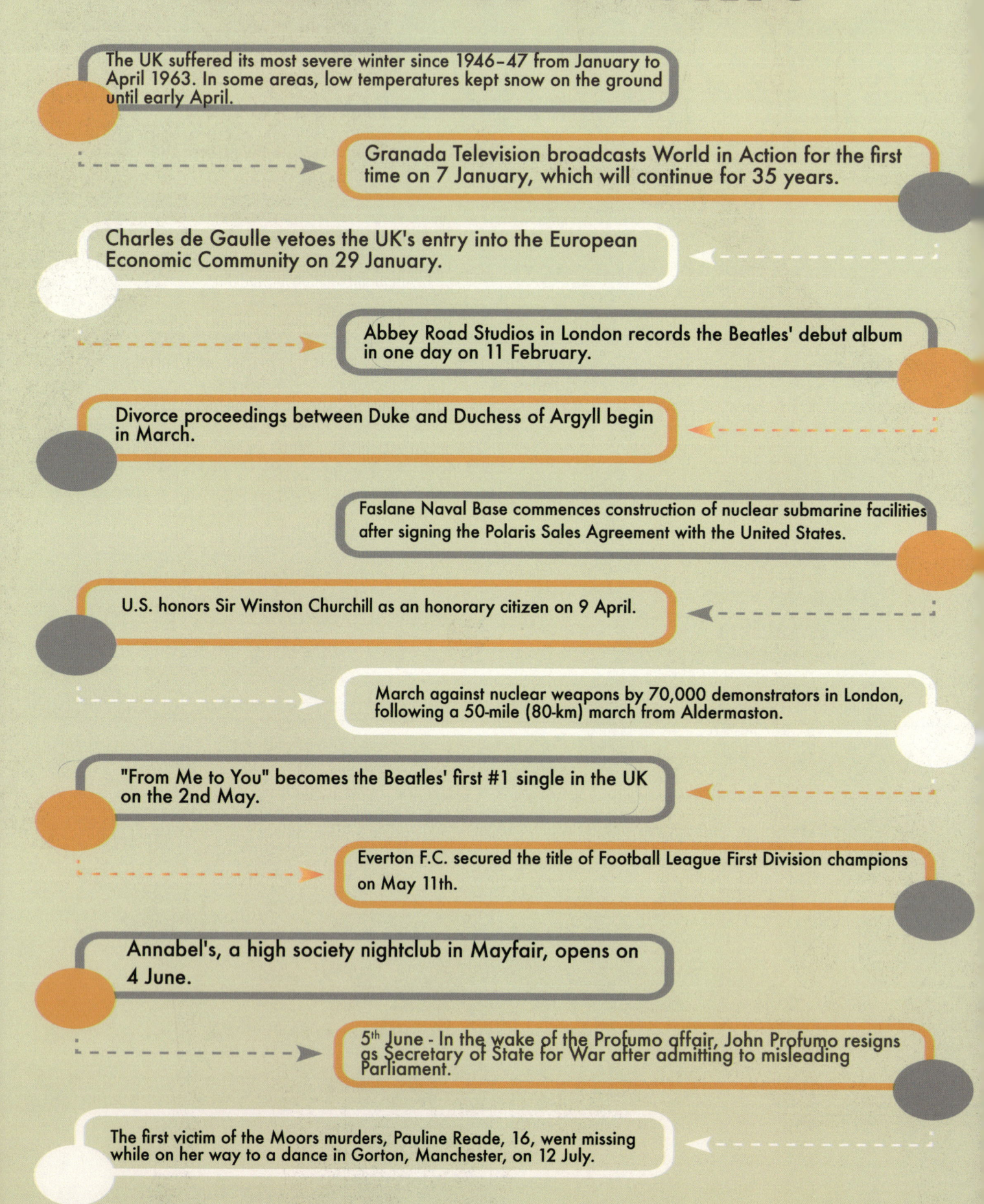

1963 UK events

- The UK suffered its most severe winter since 1946–47 from January to April 1963. In some areas, low temperatures kept snow on the ground until early April.

- Granada Television broadcasts World in Action for the first time on 7 January, which will continue for 35 years.

- Charles de Gaulle vetoes the UK's entry into the European Economic Community on 29 January.

- Abbey Road Studios in London records the Beatles' debut album in one day on 11 February.

- Divorce proceedings between Duke and Duchess of Argyll begin in March.

- Faslane Naval Base commences construction of nuclear submarine facilities after signing the Polaris Sales Agreement with the United States.

- U.S. honors Sir Winston Churchill as an honorary citizen on 9 April.

- March against nuclear weapons by 70,000 demonstrators in London, following a 50-mile (80-km) march from Aldermaston.

- "From Me to You" becomes the Beatles' first #1 single in the UK on the 2nd May.

- Everton F.C. secured the title of Football League First Division champions on May 11th.

- Annabel's, a high society nightclub in Mayfair, opens on 4 June.

- 5th June - In the wake of the Profumo affair, John Profumo resigns as Secretary of State for War after admitting to misleading Parliament.

- The first victim of the Moors murders, Pauline Reade, 16, went missing while on her way to a dance in Gorton, Manchester, on 12 July.

1963 UK events

A nuclear test ban treaty is signed by the United States, the United Kingdom, and the Soviet Union on 5 August.

In Buckinghamshire, the Great Train Robbery occurs on 8 August.

Sep. - The Sindy fashion doll is first marketed by Pedigree.

Fred Vine and Drummond Matthews publish proof of seafloor spreading in the Atlantic Ocean on 7 September.

23 September – The Robbins Report is published. According to it, universities should be expanded immediately, and university places should be available "to all who are qualified by ability and attainment".

New Viva is launched by Vauxhall on 26 September, similar to BMC's 1100 and Ford Anglia.

10th Oct - Prime Minister Harold Macmillan announces his resignation after nearly seven years in office, at the age of 69, on the grounds of ill health.

From Russia with Love, the second James Bond film, premieres at Odeon Leicester Square in London.

A 65-year-old C. S. Lewis dies in Oxford on 22 November. He is best known for his Narnia books (1950–1955).

The first episode of the BBC Television science fiction series Doctor Who was broadcast on 23rd November. William Hartnell plays the First Doctor in the show.

12 December - with Jomo Kenyatta as Prime Minister, Kenya gains independence from the United Kingdom.

Edward Craven-Walker, the founder of Mathmos, launches the Astro or lava lamp.

With GDP reaching 4.3% in the second quarter, economic growth is at a postwar high of 7.5% (slightly higher than 1959's 7.2%).

60s Inventions

Audio Cassette 1963

The Philips Company named it "Compact Cassette"

Cochlear Implants

William house invented a single-channel implant in 1961.

Fiber-Tip Pen 1962

Invented in Japan by Masoa Miura & Yukio Horie

1963 Valium Anti-Anxiety Drug.

The LED Light Emitting Diode Space Observatories, by Ball Brothers Aerospace Corp.

Lava Lamp - 1963

Lava lamps were invented by Edward Craven-Walker in 1963. During that time, he called it 'Astro Lamp'. Despite the fact that the exact formula is a secret, other companies have replicated it because lava lamps remain a popular item. As the wax melts, the floating wax in the water-based liquid rises and falls. Tetrachloride keeps the wax buoyant and heavy enough to sink.

Spacewar the first Computer Video Game - 1962

Bubble wrap

An excellent example of an accidental invention. Their goal was to create textured wallpaper. The air that kept accumulating between the plastic layers initially discouraged them. When they founded Sealed Air Corporation in 1960, they were still trying to find a viable use for this material. Little did they know that technology of another kind would provide their solution. When IBM released the 1401 computer, they needed a safe way to ship the fragile device. In an instant, they realised what their plastic air wrap should do, and the rest, as they say, is history.

Kevlar

Continuing our theme of amazing accidental discoveries, we present Poly-paraphenylene terephthalamide (Kevlar). In 1964, the company was looking for a way to make tyres that were strong but lightweight. Stephanie Kwolek created a mixture that did not have the desired attributes. After drying the mixture, Stephanie discovered that it was extremely strong. As a result, this amazing invention has saved the lives of many people since the 1960s and continues to do so.

Aspartame

Invention stories are often surprising. Chemist James M. Schlatter licked his finger to turn a piece of paper, which led to the creation of Aspartame. While working on an anti-ulcer drug, he managed to get some of the synthesized material on his hand. After discovering that it had an incredibly sweet taste, he knew it could have other uses. This wasn't approved until 1981.

Britain in the '60s

Your generation grew up in a decade marked by a cultural revolution fuelled by youth. A generation of people born in the 1940s and 1950s ignited changes in Britain. During the 1960s, we saw the impact of a generation free of conscription but who remembered the war and its scarcity.

The economy improved as technology developed, and families were able to enjoy leisure activities. The typical sixties recalled as the 'Swinging sixties' are reflective of urban cities with concentrated groups of young people involved in music, the arts, and fashion. It wasn't the everyday life most people remember, but it still played a huge role in their lives.

Teenagers were born in the fifties, but it was the 1960s when young people began to speak out. Social and economic factors have led to a heightened level of creative expression not previously possible. It was parents who wished to see their children have fun that created teenagers who were quite different from previous generations in many ways.

It can be argued that the 1960s were the most revolutionary decade of the 20th century. As employment levels increased, the economy boomed. In turn, this affected the appetite for new technology. Televisions and pocket transistor radios allowed people to listen to music and watch television shows. Colour TV licences were introduced in 1968 and cost £10 (although black & white TV sets didn't outnumber colour until 1978 due to the high price). There were fewer than 200,000 households with colour TVs in 1969 – if you owned one, you were among the lucky ones!

With the race to the moon, the thriving music scene, the British invasion and British fashion subcultures paving the way for modern design, the decade of the '60s had an air of optimism. By the end of the decade, Neil Armstrong & Buzz Aldrin achieved the impossible by becoming the first men to land on the moon (1969). Unlike the battered and bruised Britain of the 1950s, the 1960s were a time of hope and expectation of a bright future.

The Legal Stuff

All rights reserved @ Little Pips Press

Attribution for photo images goes to the following talented photographers under the creative commons licenses specified:

Attribution 4.0 International (CC BY 4.0)
Attribution-ShareAlike 4.0 International (CC BY-SA 4.0)

https://www.flickr.com/photos/89375755@N00/50207122233

https://www.flickr.com/photos/pedrosimoes7/44315585155/in/photolist-2awfXx2-2dxYoCm-

https://www.flickr.com/photos/pedrosimoes7/49982308446/in/photolist-2j9LoWJ-zDt

https://www.flickr.com/photos/51764518@N02/45189213524/in/photolist-2bRdwP7-2256Xxs-

https://www.flickr.com/photos/51764518@N02/38771477700/

https://www.flickr.com/photos/autohistorian/48435129907/in/gallery-189870699@N02-72157715885312652/

https://www.flickr.com/photos/pedrosimoes7/49982308446/in/gallery-189870699@N02-72157715885312652/

https://www.flickr.com/photos/rtw501/50298819903/in/gallery-189870699@N02-72157715885312652/

https://www.flickr.com/photos/romitagirl67/14169792817/in/gallery-189870699@N02-72157715885312652/

https://www.flickr.com/photos/romitagirl67/17271841910/in/photolist-sj

https://www.flickr.com/photos/51764518@N02/29396111524/in/photolist-LMCKP3-2gByGcM-2e5mK9s-nwo_lfh

https://www.flickr.com/photos/149233735@N05/30963568902

https://www.flickr.com/photos/91591049@N00/50043840332/

https://www.flickr.com/photos/7477245@N05/7470707808/i

https://www.flickr.com/photos/western4uk/8153200992

https://www.flickr.com/photos/28761247@N04/8285060491

https://www.flickr.com/photos/21233184@N02/4188316368

https://www.flickr.com/photos/abataphobia/5012073439/

https://www.flickr.com/photos/beatlegirl/24538568O9/in/gallery-189870699@N02-72157715885312652/

https://www.flickr.com/photos/roeshad/2038227674/in/faves-189870699@N02/

https://www.flickr.com/photos/24931020@N02/82977130068/in/faves-189870699@N02/

https://www.flickr.com/photos/amadeusrecord/5718161855/in/faves-189870699@N02/

https://www.flickr.com/photos/83706716@N02/7679736976/in/faves-189870699@N02/

Printed in Great Britain
by Amazon